Steps

A Book of Aphorisms

By

Bradley Denton Reese Jr.

This short work is dedicated to the steps Amanda Pease and I make together.

Introduction

"Jesus Christ," my father yelled as he hung tightly to the appropriately named bar on the passenger side of his Ford Expedition. My older sister Jennifer, behind the wheel of the immense gas slaughtering SUV, with me eavesdropping and day dreaming in the backseat, just ahead of me, my father's knuckles were turning white; he was surely trying to find the right words to alter his daughter's driving.

Despite the SUV's size, or because of it, whenever another car approached from the opposing lane of the Rural Route Highway 104, my sister made absolutely certain of avoiding it. We would hug the white line that guards the shoulder from fields of corn and soybean, only to finally swerve back into the middle of the right lane once the car was long passed. This wave repeated itself every time another car approached; my father's patience waning and knowing it important not to frighten an already frightened driver, he decided on the following phrase to fix the situation:

"You have to watch out for the car in front of the one behind you."

My sister's expression changed from what at first looked like a combination of apprehension and confusion into something akin to understanding. Though her eyebrows and face contortions might have fooled me, I was of course spying using the reflection on the rear view mirror, her driving did not. The lesson stuck. We stayed in the middle of the lane the rest of the way, never minding all the cars and all the troubles. Jennifer remained unwaveringly fixed on a trajectory toward home.

My father's words curbed the curvy situation and without knowing it, began my love affair with aphorisms. Defining an aphorism is tricky business. They change the way we view the horizon, kindling perspectival shifts, twists of logic, and in my sister's case, providing valuable life lessons. They lend themselves to abstraction and metaphor. My father's words mold easily from a simple lesson to a metaphysical outlook on life itself. The troubles of life are too many and too varied, just worrying about yourself is sometimes enough. And yet aphorisms do have characteristics that hold them all under one umbrella.

Aphorisms are short. They are quick. They are dance steps in thought that take us from peak to peak, only to finish with a turn, a twist, an intellectual pirouette.

In short they are brief phrases or statements which involve a turn of logic or a turn of phrase.

Like a novel with an unexpected ending, they can surprise us, shock us, and educate us in strange ways. They show us the power of words and the power of limits. At their best, these sophistic-laconic phrases show us something about ourselves, something about our limits.

Limits are horizons, so too are aphorisms. The word comes from the Ancient Greek combines *Apo* (from) with *Horos* (horizon). The combination tells us how far we can go, and sometimes how fast.

"Don't go faster than the car in front of you."

Is another of my father's driving aphorisms, at first it seems like a lesson on tailgating, but after multiple reprimands and scoldings it began to follow different path, a more philosophic path, a path into relativity. No not like Einstein relativity, more a position, based on those around you, with the world around you, with the horizon all about you.

Society tells us that there are speed limits, structures that limit our freedom on the road; additionally, there are other cars on the road, other impediments to our absolute freedom.

Initially I remember thinking that if there are no cars in front of me, wouldn't that mean I could drive as fast as I wanted? But my father again made me remember the lesson he had given Jennifer five years prior. You always have limits, some given by the state, some given by the situation, and some given by yourself. The key to driving, and to living, is knowing how to handle each turn and how to navigate each road. Aphorisms are a lesson in limits. They are quick road signs on our path, and sometimes they show us when we hit our destination.

I began this work, not knowing where it was heading, in the fall of 2014. At first it was just sitting down with a bottle of wine, the news paper, a notebook, and a pen. Ruminating on all the things I thought of saying, but never did.

The first step was turning my censor off. The little guy that tells us to be polite, to not offend, to yield, and not to conquer. With each aphorism I wrote it felt like I was taking steps towards myself.

I was being honest with myself, often staying up late laughing at the goofy things I had to say, and thinking about the provoking things that flowed from my pen.

The name of the work comes from this path. Aphorisms are dance steps in thought.

At first I was just trying to be playful and to pass the time, but eventually a mixture of repartee and regret fueled the fire. The maxim like structure of aphorisms often make them feel like they have the final word, that they capture the insurmountable hill, dominate the movie scene, and leave the room dumbfounded with their sheer cleverness. Susan Sontag, herself a natural aphorist, warns us of the particular character of the form:

"An aphorism is not an argument; it is too well-bred for that."

Pretention plays a large part in my work of aphorisms. One of my perpetual faults is to try and prove that I am the smartest person in the room. In so doing, I often prove the opposite.

But aphorisms are not about proving points. They are about asserting points. Their argument is their brevity, their matter of factness, and their aristocratic air. Vanity makes me want to be remembered, I whole heartedly agree with Friedrich Nietzsche when he claimed:

"Whoever writes in blood and aphorism wants not to be learned but to be learned by heart."

I hope that some of my quips will do just that, but at the very least, I would be happy if they just make your blood rise with anger or indignation. An interesting criterion for success, but one I am comfortable with.

Upon arranging my aphorisms I noticed certain tropes and themes, these were not planned, but seemed to creep up with the writing itself. Politics, philosophy, love, and truth seem to dominate. Not surprising really, considering those topics follow all our daily social interactions. Look out for irony, he plays a small but successful role.

However, I suspect the astute reader will find a couple of aphorisms that contradict each other. All I can say is contradictions are inherent in the tension of the work; additionally, any fool can throw a rock in a pond that ten wise men cannot find. Instead of throwing rocks, I encourage you to take to pen and pad, it is much more rewarding.

The task of reading aphorisms remains open, what is the best way to read them? Should we read them in order, or out of order? Is there even an order? To give rest to these questions I offer you the following aphorism:

"An aphorism is a link in a chain of thoughts. It demands that the reader reconstitute this chain with his own means." Friedrich Nietzsche

Unlike Nietzsche, my demand is as light as the chain of thought, there are no rules, so feel free to jump from number to number, and from page to page. The steps you take are entirely up to you.

1

A blank page longs for ink like a band-aid longs for blood.

2

No dance ever lies.

3

A fireplace is any place I start a fire.

4

The death of a tree is the life of a holiday.

5

Lightning strikes trees because its branches long to have roots.

6

No pen can draw a sword like a knight.

7

Presidents are products sold to all Americans, but only bought by a few.

8

Temptation is the only noun I know of that acts like a verb.

9

Pick up lines are for men who think woman are "objects" to "pick up."

10

Liars are just like fires, they always manage to burn themselves out.

11

The gravity of the situation depends on its weight.

12

The Framers would have done better had they actually seen our portrait.

13

I never leave anything to Chance, he always takes it.

14

Today men no longer wear capes; consequently, we no longer have heroes.

15

Books hold the key to our past and to our future; only us readers must supply the binding.

16

Life is the culmination of the lies we tell ourselves so that we can fit in, while forgetting the best of us that might have made us stand out.

17

The last step is the first step towards home.

18

I'm all for same-sex marriage, at least there is sex in it.

19

Whenever you seek change, look no further than the couch.

20

Who takes pictures of the Milky Way galaxy?

21

If two roads diverge into a yellow wood, just wait for one of them to turn green.

22

Literally doesn't literally mean literally anymore.

23

I can never find the app on my phone that is supposed to help me find my other apps.

24

I'll never buy pepper spray again, it made my steak taste like shit.

25

The only thing cheap in Las Vegas is yourself.

26

A woman always shows herself – barely.

27

Never trust a person whose kite is always up in the wind.

28

Does it matter that all we are is dead star matter?

29

Whenever leading, cover up your tracks.

30

"Do not tell, show." The maxim of all writers and pedophiles.

31

A life in front of the bar is a life behind bars.

32

We all must walk the beat, if nobody is policing the police.

33

All corn is maize, but not all maize is corn, except in a corn maze.

34

The right way to die is to leave nothing left.

35

Who among us has the strength to kill our Founding Fathers, who among us has the strength to be a Revolutionary Mother?

36

The limits of your horizon are your horizon.

37

Thinking over every second makes for a long day.

38

Tornadoes are jumping justice.

39

The only thing worse than having nothing to say – is saying it.

40

A falcon that remembers his falconer forgets his freedom.

41

I wonder what sin caused the star to fall.

42

If there is a wall between you and you-R-self, it depends on who you R.

43

The worse thing about Whole Foods is that you can never find the Half & Half.

44

A man never quite reaches his target, but a dart at least leaves a mark.

45

Never sweep dust under a rug, forever it will sleep.

46

If icebergs are so deep, how come they can float?

47

The squeaky wheel gets the oil, but the silent protester gets shot.

48

If you marry for looks, you'll see what you deserve.

49

Don't overcook your noodle, or it will turn into mush.

50

It is always your turn when you are on point.

51

Democracy ends in violence, begins in violence, and the rest is tyranny.

52

Do we call each other brothers and sisters because we have lost our fathers and mothers?

53

Those who are kool look different, because they are indifferent to the way they look.

54

I found the truth the other day, it was in the last place I looked.

55

If love requires space, I'll take the edge.

56

Why run with scissors when you can skip with grenades?

57

If the undead are, are the are, dead? (A Zombie-Kantian Parable)

58

Wine, the only thing worth bottling up.

59

The smell of pine, so warm in life, so cold in death.

60

Lupus is a wolf that never howls at the moon.

61

I always fail to say the truth, except for this one time.

62

It's not one broken string that kills a man – it's a string of them.

63

You never fly a kite in Chicago – it flies you.

64

Gamblers believe the universe was randomly put there for them.

65

Never trust a woman in leggings, she has lost the art of concealment.

66

How come we know about the Secret Service?

67

The toilet bowl reminds us of where we have been, the smell tells us when it is time to go.

68

Nothing is louder than a dead protestor.

69

Time is the justice of our jails; jails are the injustice of our time.

70

Voting only serves to prevent the voice of the people from becoming violent.

71

The best way to forget something is placing it in context: museums for art, memorials for war, and tombstones for men.

72

Protests start to fail as soon as they start to win.

73

Remember when our government bailed on Main Street to bail out Wall Street – don't worry nobody else does either.

74

The correct way to end a lifelong argument – is suicide.

75

The only difference between swimming and drowning is success.

76

Sirens never sing twice.

77

Now – racecar – won.

78

Relationships are the only time one plus one equals three.

79

A writer is interested in everything and no one.

80

Flash mobs are never spontaneous.

81

Some balls never get their bearings.

82

Serious jokers are hard to find.

83

Nothing hurts the image of Muhammad, like the violence done in his name.

84

No drone ever kills an innocent on accident.

85

Scabs never worry about being picked on.

86

Confidence is never lying to yourself, but always to others.

87

Chivalry isn't dead, it's just that there are too many boys.

88

"Word of mouth," is there any other kind?

89

The tragedy of the promise of politics is that it requires tragedy.

90

Future dictionaries will substitute sharing pictures for sharing love.

91

Man is the only triangle that can no longer support himself.

92

There is nothing more dangerous than an action done out of regret.

93

Plato was not a Platonist, Christ was not a Christian, Kant was not a Kantian, Nietzsche was not a Nietzschean, Heidegger was not a Heideggerian, Strauss was not a Straussian, Derrida was not a Derridean. The history of philosophy shows us one thing: a thinker is separate from his thought.

94

Philosophers shift paradigms, thinkers just tinker, but unlucky for us scholars always remember.

95

He who has a lamp in his hand, can see through any dark.

96

Screens are the screaming streaming light of our time, at what temperature will these weapons of mass distraction kindle, spark, and burn?

97

Capitalism extols that man is the master of his fate, but as Aristotle claimed, "Man alone is either a beast or a God," it is then fitting today that capitalism is both.

98

Attraction is the illusion of mutual reception.

99

No new flame ever completely goes out, it just finds different places to burn.

100

The last president worth remembering probably wrote his own speeches.

101

Is terrorism the only form of political action today?

102

Each time a philosopher claims to have the truth, they kill philosophy. The search for truth is an erotic act, ultimately without climax.

103

I am not sad because I am here alone, but because you are there alone.

104

Boredom is a boon: Distraction is a disease.

105

Never trust a Democrat who does not lock his door.

106

If someone asks you, "What class do you belong to?" Your answer depends on whether or not you take a shower before or after work.

107

Management is waiting.

108

Is it possible for us today to have a fiction, which we know to be a fiction, but a fiction we nonetheless believe in? If the answer is no, the promise of politics is over.

109

Storms remind us that it's better to lean against something, than to stand against nothing.

110

If President Lincoln's warning that a house divided against itself cannot stand was correct, then why did our Founding Fathers insist upon a bicameral legislature?

111

Ice that falls on the rich, never fails.

112

Some men cry, Some men lie, All men live, if only to die.

113

Democrats forget that puppies and little children cannot vote: Republicans forget that woman can.

114

Aphorisms are to aristocracy : as tweets are to democracy. One requires conception, the other a mere connection.

115

If every snowflake is unique, how come we call them all snowflakes?

116

I can only believe in a man who has won and lost a war with himself.

117

You choose to be indecisive.

118

My best letters are those left unsent, filed away in a size eleven truth filled shoebox.

119

There is no terror like a terrorist who happens to agree with you, but who manages to do something about it.

120

I hope the kids of my future never know about the kid of my past.

121

Securing extreme economic inequality – The only Republican Party platform ever.

122

Occupy Wall Street might have changed the space of our future had they decided to blow up the banks of our past and our present.

123

"There will be no smoking on this train," … "That's good cause I'm inside the train."

124

I'd rather gain the discipline learned to do something considered useless by politicians (i.e. self appointed educational curriculum experts), like say learning cursive or playing the flute, than spend my days preparing for standardized tests, which are only useful to lawmakers in helping them quantify school performance and school funding. If your school does poorly, instead of allocating more funds, better teachers, and more resources, you'll find your federal funding revoked. Thereby perpetuating the cycle of inequality, the better schools get better, the bad schools get worse.

The absence of cursive is a symptom of the absence of common sense in the common core curriculum. The only measure of our lawmakers success is our own American educational failure.

125

The best tragedy enables me to commit fake suicide.

126

The best comedy enables me to laugh at my certain death.

127

Birds can always find their way home and
scientists reason it is in the bird's brain. I
believe it is in their flight, in their movement, in
their perpetual dance with the wind.

128

We cannot control it, fix it, or understand it.
Nature is not organic, but chaotic.

129

Do not disturb me while I am reading. You
wouldn't stop a person while they were mowing
the lawn, surely, reading is just as important as
cutting grass.

130

All my favorite writers have the decency of
never giving me any sympathy.

131

A good writer is a poor writer who didn't quit.

132

If philosophy is learning how to die, then poetry
is learning how to cope.

133

The powerful ignore education in favor of pure propaganda.

134

Taboo & Sexuality : Fear & Fuel.

135

An aphorism is a lesson in high and low, a lesson in levels.

136

Saying, "thank you," while working in customer service sometimes is a polite way of saying, "go fuck yourself."

137

No one with a full heart can make room for another to love them with all their heart.

138

You cannot stand on a timetable.

139

Depression always leaves a mark.

Bradley Denton Reese Jr.

140

Something either has momentum or hasn't
there is no such thing as gathering momentum.

141

Where do all the abandoned dreams go?

142

America's indifference is more violent than any
riot.

143

Life is simply the collision of what is and what
is not possible. The foolish and the reasonable
only disagree on the date of impact.

144

I returned my dancing shoes when they
couldn't dance on their own.

145

Democrats understand everything that we do
not : Republican understand nothing that we
do.

146

8's are just two 3's making love.

147

A man who sits on everything, stands for nothing.

148

I always take the time to leave promptly.

149

Statistics are what speculative investors use on Wall Street to gamble away your retirement money.

150

No racist ever completely ignores the rhetorical power of statistics.

151

Insanity is the momentary burden of individual insight; we used to call it by another name: revelation.

152

Words are the only fluid things that we can stick on other fluid things.

153

Truth is never clean; it often lies in bed with fleas, and wakes up with lies.

154

A nightmare is a dream come true.

155

American Intellectual – a perfect oxymoron.

156

Truth is not about finding correctness or correspondence. That would be like debating over the scientific taxonomy of a fish you caught that morning in the lake, instead of just being thankful for your fucking dinner.

157

The value of your degree depends on your temperature.

158

Unlearning is the only true education.

159

Ignore the roots of the problem – you'll soon find your trees on fire.

160

Fake memories are just as strong as real ones.

161

The only way to fix the cable is to cut it.

162

No Turkey remembers Thanksgiving.

163

On Irony

It is said that irony can be a form of dogmatism. And yet, it is true that fundamentalist dictators are never ironic. They are dogmatic tyrants. Does irony have a peculiar form of tyranny running through its threads?

Irony relies on the tyranny of rank. The magnanimous man uses irony so as to not offend those beneath him, while speaking to those equal with him. His irony is a form of courtesy. This idea of hierarchal irony sounds foreign to us twenty-first century egalitarian intellectuals, because we are now deaf to the sound of ironies peculiar benefits. It can be a form of teaching, it can blend high and low into a meaningful whole, it can preserve the high for those worthy of it, and maintain the low for those who need it.

Irony is a method of in and out, who gets the joke, and who doesn't. It both makes and mends walls. It protects us from the dogmatic draft of democracy, while at the same time reminding us of the possibility of aristocratic greatness. This form of tyranny is well worth preserving, at least ironically.

164

My tongue is my iceberg.

165

I've found my happiest moments are when I am lost in the moment.

166

Life is a check signed under the influence; consequently, it is hardly ever worth saving.

167

There are no existential problems. Do not worry whether the glass is half full or half empty, just be thankful for the fucking water.

168

Do not get upset when others cannot climb your walls, instead just lower your bridge.

169

Meaning is not man made, it is made for man.

170

We are constantly running away from death, but are forever shocked when it manages to find its way home.

171

I kill pleasure, and it kills me.

172

Learning to forgive your enemies, that is nothing compared to learning to forgive yourself.

173

Does depression last longer in some people because they are more cut out for it?

174

An actor is just a fancy word for a professional waiter, or perhaps a professional president.

175

The ice on your chest never shakes when it melts, but you do.

176

Man is dead, and modern man has killed him.

177

Earth is utopia, literally no place for man, yet at the same time our place.

178

Is it better to shock, thank be shocking? Is it better to provoke, than be provoking? Is it better to truth, than to be truthing? What is truthing? Don't you know by now?

179

The only religions that I believe to be true are the ones I know to be false.

180

A scientist : a secular priest. They both want control, they both have one master, yet neither has the strength to become master. Instead they took the modest route of "truth teller" or "fable pusher."

181

Media: there to make you judge the oppressed and forget the rest.

182

They say that truth makes the unfamiliar, familiar. Truth is the nuclear family we are forever orphaned from.

183

If you believe that words "have" meaning, you probably still think that people do too. We do not "have" meaning, we are meaning.

184

Do all lives matter to rocks?

185

A fresh talk about race relations is another way to not talk about economic inequality.

186

Some goals begin and end with guilt.

187

I wonder what roots the tree of knowledge must have.

188

Knowledge is not power, truth is not power, ignorance is not power. Power marks everything with its own currency.

189

The lightness of comedy comes from the
darkness of life.

190

Are you lying to yourself, thank god, for once,
you are being honest.

191

Pain: what people often get if they think that
happiness is about pleasure.

192

Life is not the pursuit of happiness, but rather
the pursuit of something worth suffering for.

193

Being a better teacher requires being a better
slave toward yourself.

194

Moralistic language should be deaf to the sound
of truth.

195

Violence is the only voice left to those who
cannot be heard.

196

Do not confuse truth with living, lies with living, entertainment with living, your life with living.

197

Are has nothing to do with truth: it doesn't capture it, enliven it, or showcase it. Art is us – We are not truth.

198

Humans are the animals that have forgotten their hands and teeth, and substituted their "reason" and "truth."

199

"And yet I think it better, my good friend, that my lyre should be discordant and out of tune, and any chorus I might train, and that the majority of mankind should disagree with and oppose me, rather than that I, who am but one man, should be out of tune with myself (Plato's Gorgias 282; cf Aristotle's Metaphysics Book Gamma 3-6)."

The origin of the only truth to come out of philosophy: the principle of non-contradiction.

200

Seeing what is close is more important than seeing what is past.

201

Politics is where men go to fuck up our lives, and woman who aren't their wives.

202

The best conversations often never take place.

203

Keeping quiet is the key to any great conversation.

204

It is not that you say too much, but rather that my ears can only hold a little.

205

If a relationship was easy it wouldn't be meaningful, it would just be an engagement.

206

With family, I always feel unfamiliar to myself.

207

Do not mistake your lovers smile for their heart.

208

A chance meeting is like a taste of a future fate you won't have.

209

The best love is always a stranger, new each day.

210

Some love the love, some love the lover, some love themselves, and some, the best, just love another.

211

The only poets today are writing copy of advertising firms.

212

A banana doesn't care what color it is.

213

Riots are not the root of the problem, they are merely the trees that have grown too tall for cutting.

214

It is truth universally acknowledged, that a man in possession of a wife, is in want of good fortune. (Contra Jane Austen)

215

Who is the captain of this relation-ship?

216

A person who keeps the inside of their apartment clean, only cares how it looks to people from the outside.

217

Cats are a constant reminder of the point of life.

218

If you stare at the sun long enough you become blind, but if you stare at the dark long enough, you can see.

219

The Civil Rights Movement success was its ultimate failure. It became part of the system that was the problem.

220

Dying for something doesn't make it true.

221

Death takes us all, what matters is what we leave.

222

Whenever you get rid of those demon prejudices, beware, perhaps you just threw out some angels.

223

Everyone has a novel inside of them, and that is precisely where it ought to remain.

224

I stand on the shoulders of giants, and can see nothing through the clouds. (Contra Sir Isaac Newton).

225

You can rest assured that my vengeance will never rest.

226

It takes two rails for one track, and two tracks for one rail.

227

The square grid system of streets makes it easy
to get around.

228

A fist, the best way to stop a quarrel before it
starts.

229

Birds do not make good ornithologists: humans
do not make good anthropologists.

230

Learning something by heart lasts longer than
learning something by rote.

231

Ninjas only wear silent flip-flops.

232

The soul: breath & touch.

233

Mistakes are costly when the stakes are high.

234

I'd rather have dinner with an out-law than an in-law.

235

Satellite television rests on the orbit of the inept around the planet platitude.

236

The only thing better than the first drink is the next one.

237

The high time for brunch is before noon.

238

The best thing about aristocracy is that you know who your great grandparents were, and for some reason that fucking matters.

239

The older I get the wiser my father becomes.

240

A lie sounds better when it is sound, a truth sounds better when it is found.

241

It is easier to be fairly honest than to be honest fairly.

242

I've never seen a progressive idea that didn't eventually evolve into a conservative one.

243

My least favorite thing about freedom of speech is how rare I hear it.

244

Boom box was the name we had for the well known village lady.

245

Yeast never commits suicide in vain.

246

There is freedom of the press, but never freedom from the press.

247

The violent act that sparks a revolution later serves to prevent future revolutions.

248

They say justice can only occur among equals, doesn't it depend on who is counting.

249

What is the soul? Nothing more than what the world will take from you.

250

Management in retail is two parts self loathing, two parts nagging, and four parts bullshit.

251

A hangover reminds us that actions have consequences.

252

No amount of legislation can fix the trap of being born in a particular time and in a particular place.

253

Extemporaneous remarks require years of training.

254

If black absorbs all colors how come we can see it?

255

Apathy is pathetic.

256

The only thing I learned in confirmation camp was how to say the word "no."

257

Ovens never pre-heat, they just heat.

258

I have never seen a train arrive On time, but just In time.

259

I can never keep my numbers in order.

260

Aphorisms are dance steps in thought.